AN AUDIBLE BLUE

AN AUDIBLE BLUE

Selected Poems (1963–2016)

Klaus Merz

Translated from the German
and with an introduction by
Marc Vincenz

WHITE PINE PRESS \ BUFFALO, NEW YORK

White Pine Press
P.O. Box 236
Buffalo, NY 14201
www.whitepine.org

Selections in this book were all published in Klaus Merz's collected works: *Die Lamellen Stehen Offen: Frühe Lyrik 1963–1991* (2011), Band 1; *Außer Rufweite: Lyrik 1992–2013* (2013), Band 7; and the stand-alone collection, *Helios Transport* (2016), all by Haymon Verlag, Innsbruck, Austria. A list of the original poems and their respective first-edition publications can be found in the continuation of the copyright page on page 258.

Publication of this book was supported by a grant from by public funds from the New York State Council on the Arts, with the support of Governor Kathy Hochul and the New York State Legislature, a State Agency; with a grant from ProHelvetia, the Swiss Arts Council, and with funds from the Amazon Literary Partnership.

SWISS ARTS COUNCIL

prohelvetia

Printed and bound in the United States of America.

Book design: Elaine LaMattina

Cover art: Jack Zulli, "See the Sound." Copyright © 2022 by Jack Zulli.

ISBN 978-1-945680-54-0

Library of Congress Control Number: 2021941426

Contents

I. THE GILLS ARE WIDE OPEN (1963–1991)

White-Hot Thoughts: Uncollected Poems 1963–1967

With Collective Blindness (1967)

Debris of My Country (1969)

II. OUT OF EARSHOT (1992–2003)

Breath. Pneumnia. Foehn.

Lion Lions: Reflections of Venice (2004)

Out of the Dust (2010)

Dream Leftovers

Big Business

Helios Hauls (2016)

AN AUDIBLE BLUE

Cigarettes, Celestial Bodies
and the Truckers' Union

The majority of this selection of Klaus Merz's poems, with the exception of those in *Helios Hauls* (2016), was distilled from Volumes 1 and 7 of his collected works (1963–2013), published by the Austrian, Innsbruck-based Haymon Verlag. A complete list of all original poems and their respective first-edition publications is acknowledged on page 258. His 2,352-page collected works include poetry, novellas, short stories and essays. For fifty years' writing, Merz's oeuvre may seem relatively slim, yet from very early on (in his early twenties) Merz has been a master of the short form—both in his poetry and his fiction. Many of his poems run only three or four lines, reminiscent of haiku or perhaps the Taoist poets of the eighth century. And one of Merz's great gifts as a writer is his facility with condensation, distillation and concision, not just in his very considered word choices, but also in precisely what he decides to leave out of the story. One gets the sense that each of his word choices are considered and reconsidered a hundred times; and I do know that the earliest poems were sculpted from a large piece of stone, moving inward, until he finally had his kernel, whereas in more recent times, he builds outward, weighing each word as he writes. And thus, too, Merz's poems are to be devoured slowly, and require many readings. Indeed, even in what on the surface seems a simple seven-line poem about a trip to Russia from Merz's 1995 collection *Short Announcement*, we begin with an image of a toothless elephant:

> *A toothless elephant*
> *stares into the skylight.*

The toothless elephant serves not only as a stand-in for the piano, which only appears on line five, but also as a reminder of where the keys originally came from. The dodecaphonist, a practitioner of the twelve-tone technique—a rather dramatic sound which avoids the composition being fixed to any one key—appears in the third line:

> *The dodecaphonist raps*
> *her fingers on the desk.*

Obviously the piano itself is missing, and we soon discover

> *The piano has been pawned.*

At this stage, the reader may well be wondering why the poem is entitled, "A Russian Trip," but by the sixth line we are all fighting for the last droplets of soup:

> *We ladle out the soup*
> *fearlessly fast.*

In a short poem of seven lines, the poem opens up into the brutal reality that was Yeltsin's elephant in the room: food shortages, economic volatility and inflation.

*

In many of Merz's poems there is clear narrative drive, and much of it is gleaned from everyday experience in the Swiss countryside where he grew up and continues to thrive, but also from his journeys around the world as a Swiss looking backward. Perhaps it is here, in his overland (real or imagined) journeys to places like Tibet or Oklahoma that he finds a cross-cultural resonance in the commonality of the folk he has known all his life. Although Merz sees the world through the eyes of an almost purposeful, sometimes ironic, parochial perspective, he finds a resonance in human experience that could equally apply to any one of his countrymen or that of another culture entirely. He seeks and sees common ground in humanity and focuses on the minutiae of, say, a Swiss engineer or a German bartender, in the glances of a Venetian skipper or an Anatolian shepherd, to convey this universality.

Humor and irony figure in much of his work, and one cannot help but think that, much like Kafka, he is chuckling to himself as he writes these poems. The humor, however, is not purely for entertainment or personal amusement, but to shine a spotlight on transformative moments of human experience—much of the time in the mundane and/or the sticky little moments of worldly experience. At times these experiences become magical, and illuminate something well beyond the everyday. For example, in the poem, "Nocturnal Harvest," from the 2013 collection *Unexpected Development*, Merz gives us a view of the Big Dipper dipping:

> *Driveshaft at the fore*
> *the Big Dipper plunges*
> *toward Earth,*
> *the cart sparkles.*

And here, as he stares into the night sky, he intervenes in the celestial with a cigarette:

> *With the glow of my cigarette*
> *I guide it home.*

Or, in his poem, "Moody February," from 2016's *Helios Hauls*, two butterflies arrive early and deceive us into believing that spring is near, while

> *On the park bench*
> *a pensioner melts away.*

Or, in the poem, "Migration," from the same collection, Merz and his grandson decide that

> *We want to live*
> *on Saturn, it also*
> *serves as a carousel.*

As Merz himself has said, the vision that he has attempted to develop for a lifetime is to discover the expansive in the minuscule and the minute in the vast, and somehow to bring them into focus through the lives and mores of very normal, everyday people:

"It is imperative to embrace both close proximity and limitless distance, to edge closer in order to be able to push away forcefully again."

From a poet and translator's perspective, it has been a great honor to dig into the corners of Klaus Merz's compact yet razor-sharp mind. The act of translating him has given me insight into the absolute power of each and every individual word both in German and in English.

—Marc Vincenz
Cheshire, MA
May 2022

I.

THE GILLS ARE WIDE OPEN
(1963–1991)

White-Hot Thoughts

Uncollected Poems 1963–1967

On the Way

Close together,
the skinless fingers
of our wings
are ingrown.
In such a fashion
we swim and fly
without question toward
unspoken horizons.

Song

Hollow, the gold passing
through hands during the day.
He who rises·from light
into the shaft,
plumbs emptiness.

He finds us above
where you pay
in copper and paper.
Where silence is sawed in two
and the echo is chased away.

Jetsam

The sun washes up,
a system ruptures.

A brackish mouth
speaks to the dead.

But a new celestial body
rolls in with the next wave.

September (I)

The bloody light of the moon
drops from the branches,
falls on the shoulders,
drips into the mouth.

While resting under the tree
a sweetness gathers sanguine on the tongue,
the dark fruit
leaks another summer.

I collect the pupils
of unknown folk
and play marbles
on the mirrors of sprawling salons.

Alongside the grand festivities
brown and blue eyes roll.
As the Paleozoic falls, so too my heart,
through all the mirrors and into loneliness.

In My House

A hot hand
rests on my knee,
and when evening arrives
I have had enough of stories;
the true and the concocted
(the latter I love the best),
or not spoken at all;
yet somehow you can't get around
those words,
those checkered lying dogs
baring teeth, softly
gapless and scrappy.

You can't rely on any bite;
only Hanni's dentures
clattered so amusingly
when she served us tidbits
and pocketed the tips
with her death-soiled hands;
she had her asthma, and I
the short breaths of a scribbler.

I don't enjoy telling stories.
I'd just say "let's play marbles,"
and we thought back
or just zipped it:
torment was good
for red-headed Hans;
he died far too soon
during an autumn when the tires piled up.
The earth got away with it,
and the burial was beautiful.

Don't talk of autumns,
let the spring groan;
sweating in summer
makes it easier
to hold water—
and with a mouthful of beer,
drunken rants, summer speeches
all along the beach and
into the sea foam.

Then autumn again,
and icy winter;
we scatter salt
not to slip.
The snails died long ago
during those feasts.

In the whorl house
it's deathly quiet and dark.

The Incident

Actually nothing really happens,
even when the hair stylist moves
the parting from left to right,
everything remains old-fashioned,
and the old gents mostly
have no parting anymore,
just a crown
manicured with a razor;
the apprentice's cut,
in the hand and in the blood;
the blood looked warm
and flowed with a rush,
and the men were powerful;
they laughed with broad faces
that swallowed their eyes;
the old hole was a mouth
on those browned surfaces
beloved by the teeth,
the yellowed, decaying
gaps, and with their dentures
they said "hot-blooded,"
and rattled faster, rumbling
dribble by dribble
against the elbow,
held up by the wristband—
just the breadth
of a branching blood-network
from the hand to the watch:

At half-past three, the two held firm
on its date display: second of April,
a Saturday, good weather,
and that echoing laughter

while my hand was bleeding
disturbed the peace
just as the blade was trembling
between the fingers
of this terrified boy.

He let them sink,
laid the razor on the table,
formed a trough
with his healthy hand,
squeezed the shimmering red back inside,
but wore his loose thread
on the outside.

With Collective Blindness

1967

At Night

At night, a fear
of my hands growing
far apart led my
mother to press them
together over time.
The forgotten,
the prized apart,
crucified hands
of cracked arches.
Who might stretch a word between
the lost *Our Father*
of those estranged hands.

Toward the Newer Years

Immeasurable the land.
The wind sleeps in your tracks,
sleeping beyond recognition.
Sharpen your eyes.
The shadows multiply
with every footfall,
and the light is on fire between them.
Sharpen your eyes.
Measure every space with all your eyes.
Don't believe the wind
he lies
in ambush in old troughs and trenches.
Cast off.
The tracks fade.
The barge latches on
to the words of the fishes.

The Early Hours

The waves crash harder
toward morning; be vigilant,
collect your nets,
the gold-wrought, loosen
and hang the cords
in the wind
like a dream
of angelhair.

A rope is sturdier.

Unbutton the early day,
the vultures circle,
the moon hangs low,
and upon the hills
the sun lounges in bed.

In the twilight
between the tides,
once more I cast
my net over you.

Fly off, fly off,
fly into my eye.

Shipwreck

Massive
the ocean tonight,
and mute.

From the mussels,
harvest the eyes
like pearls

and beat
noiselessly
on the banks of stars.

In the dawn we hoist
the flag of death
over the shipwrecks.

Under the eyelids
it burns of salt.

Debris of My Country

1969

The Return

He will arrive
on the curve of a scar

with widened arms
on the inflamed tightrope,

from the sore point to the very spot
the milestones crumble,

until the tollgates
rise everywhere.

Ice Age

Rubble spills
silently through my country,
alluvium grows
from within.

The trees fall
as dugouts,
dreams sleep
in the stone.

I build my house
out of fossil remains
and embed myself deep
in the chalk,

and at the sign
of a weathered hand,
I break under pressure
into the icy landscape.

Four Façades Do Not Make a House

1972

Before the Hour

Moses, the desert fox, lives.
He never stopped
appearing before his people,
tirelessly
speaking with his hands
and talking of God,
the wrath and the righteousness,
of a god who becomes a man,
and of a man who becomes a god.

He stands and preaches
from all four corners of the earth,
and praises a promised land
from beyond the drought
and stomps with his feet.
He steps in for his people
whom he loves more than himself.

Moses never died.
He just switched his name.
The legend of the bulrushes and the miracles.
His sons still blow the trumpets
and at any hour it may happen
that they stand before Jericho
and the world,
and the world of the promised land .
crumbles to dust.

Evenings

Swapping out the stars
with a living room,
stopping by or coming home,
seated at a table
swirling in the aroma
of mandarin oranges,
a pool of light
and smoke—
that's dangerous:
deceptions cease;
veils are lifted, then dropped;
striptease is imaginable.
False sense of distance
from her to you,
shades drawn between
horizons,
walls.
But you aren't sick,
you're just tired, and sleepy,
fall asleep.
Behind your eyelids
the distances return,
then voices,
and she sings.
The unheard of becomes audible,
visible occurrences
mingle
and entangle.

Port City

At the waterfront
under glimmering pinheads,
the city sleeps.

You imagine
a sleeper
under every streetlamp,
then add the mirrored lights:
the sleeper in the surf,
her oceanic hair
at the foot of the water lantern.

But in the morning,
the lights are extinguished
and you look over
at the quarry on the mountain.

Lead lives in the ocean,
and on a lock of seaweed.

Execution

On the horizon,
beyond the dark green forest teeth,
midday broke open,
swam toward you in whitish clouds.

The whiteout from the leafage
on my work desk
(it held on to me),
the corners jabbed me,
sharp and gnawing.

I understood
that it meant
I should free my throat
and sink my hands into the earth.

Career Advice

Look ahead,
become a butcher, my child,
he understands
the entrails, knows
where to hit the mark,
and nail it.

And he quenches his thirst
with blood,
more unslakable
from victim to victim.

Soon the stalls
will be empty, my child,
then we'll move into the houses
where it will be warm.

Axiom

He who falls out of the frame
is no longer in the picture

that he made him-
self by himself.

Metamorphosis

Since we've lost
our roots, apparently
wings have grown,
and also the moth
we hatched
soars away.

Closing Sale

Still fluttering
on the balcony,
the winter skin of the previous year,
your yellowed frock of metaphors.

Time to take it down
before the first snow falls,
the snow that fills
those pockets with cold.

Shift

At seven o'clock, the sun
rests over the smokestacks,
tumbles into enormous furnaces,
jumps out of form
for the first time at eight,
red and snatched up with long pincers,
fiery little sun mirrored in my eyes,
beneath my cinched eyelid
nothing enters
and nothing comes out—
far too hot that fire, and too old.

Hard to bear that glow
when she rolls in in the morning
and hangs around until evening, her descent
behind the mountain, the forest, the lake.

Hard to bear, that recollection of light
in someone else's singed hands.

Evening after evening
they are convicted, the children,
when they return
from the woods
with those withering flowers
and that dead deer,
when they slip silently into their rooms
and slide the forest-day under their small beds.

With earth-gathering hands
they stand in court.
A sentence is passed as always.
The children bite down on the fruit.

Quietly, we carry them sleeping outside,
then return to those unfinished halves
and chomp with closed eyes, until done.

Summer's End

During parched days at the forked
tongue of midday,
my skin calls upon me to flee.

Over the bridge of her nose,
inbound, she wanders off
without a sail,
without a flag,
compressed and soaked
by the heat,
turns me inside out,
twists my innards into the light,
lets them carburize.
The smoke rises all the way to the fields,
and from the acrid walls
the thirteenth psalm resounds:
I should sing to the Lord
that he may grant me goodness.

Dry Goods

1978

Poetry

Poems
scribbled on petals,
embossed on the underside
of pink dentures.

Poems
etched on the smooth walls
of metal pistons,
as tattoos, poked
into the pubic areas of beautiful women.

Poems
candied on a thin wafer,
baked into bread,
even on work days.

Poems
legible as mirror-writing
in the beauty parlor,
in the veil of a pregnant bride.

Poems
smeared on the underside
of yolky pedestrian lines,
to be deciphered on bridge pylons
at low tide.

Poems
in the plumage of the birds left behind,
beneath the wicked tails
of scattering cats.

Poems
where they are least expected.

Poems
on the road, infiltrating,
where they can't be protected.

Beautiful Expectation

The whole day
they play war
in the woods.

But not one
of the low-flying aircraft
crash-lands in the garden.

The cider gets murky and tepid:
they have scouted out
the parachuting pilot.

It gets serious
for the fly in the glass: she drowns.

Life Learned in a Figure of Speech

As a child,
I learned fear
when we played
with matches, when
we watched the news—
by dinnertime
we'd lost our appetites.

I learned to
notch my tally stick,
and to admire anyone
who had not
invented gunpowder.

And, as the fifth wheel,
I learned how to re-
cycle.

Makeup Removal

When, at night,
in front of the mirror,
you remove your beard—
and with your toupee unhooked,
your eyeliner stripped,
I would love to meet you,

sometime at night,
in the mirror,
one face to another.

Seasons

It's autumn again,
it has been said.
But every year
an assortment of foliage
lands at my feet.

It's the evergreen
that puts the fear of God into me.

Funeral Service

In the gallery,
the organist rolls
his Sisyphus rock
on a deep A—
A-minor, abysmal grief:

Death March

But colorful glances
eye the holier-
than-thou from the wings
of the choir:

Dogs Should Live Forever

Embedded in the solo,
the mourners too,
are framed in black
all the way under their eyelids.

Bring Me the Head of Alfredo García

Fatty, leafy green
in the wreaths
and in the elegiac valley-voices
of the association's honored members.

Four Hands for a Hallelujah

Behind the black chintz,
the laughter of the flag bearers clatters about,
spraying the church windows in the cemetery
with their whiff.

Once Upon a Time in the West

Wurlitzer grief
halved under the crucifix.

Life on the Land

1982

Old Wives' Summer

On the Cadillac-chrome,
the sun glimmers
more guilelessly than ever.

Brush the wasps from the morning,
brush them under the table.
Trust your luck
until evening;

at least until the inflamed nipples of your lover
find their way back to themselves;
and, at this train station, the head conductor
with the swollen eyes is the first
to step out of the reserved section.

Life on the Land

I.

Rain expected in the evening.
In front of my window,
the youngest carpenter's son
trusses his roof-work.
He lords on his beams
and stares into the valley.
His father places a see-through nightdress
on the young bride's chaise longue.
I would love to be there
when she has it on, he says,
drawing smoke into his lungs.
To this day, the old man has already sacrificed
three fingers to the singing saw,
two right, one left.
His six grandchildren play in the garden
with a posse of black cats:
skid marks on the thoroughfare,
but the color of the school satchels
becomes more cheerful year to year.
Wait. Watch. Walk.
Love life, live longer,
The children sing in the choir.
Mother stands on the edge of the rose garden
and sweats.

Always be prepared!
The garbage man
airs out his scout's hat,
checks the wind with his wet index finger.
Today it will arrive before the evening news.
The rest of the requirements
are satisfied by the mail-order company in B__ .

II.

Early evening
at the train station,
and two adolescent boys
buy a one-way ticket to Marseille.
The conductor issues the tickets
in his best hand.
The sun shines
into the ticket office.
Six shots are loaded,
aimed,
fired!
At the shooting range, the contest
is already underway.
From above, the flagpole
salutes the fatherland.
Foehn wind as always
when targets are so near.
The shooters shake
the carpenter's father's
unwavering hand.
A grandson has stuck
both his fingers in his ears.
I can feel the shots in my womb,
says the woman at the drinks stand.
The son of an Anatolian shepherd with his flock
circles the edge of the fairground
entirely unnoticed.

III.

At last, the editor of the *Valley Wind Weekly*
lies, run over at the curb,
his fisheye blinks in the sun;
on his face, a scrap of his newspaper,
slowly stains red.
In front of the terrace of the asylum,
north of the village
someone is radioing jokes to Sicily.
Non capisco, amico, is transmitted back.
He tries to reach Greenland
but no one is home.
All of my friends rest in the ether,
snickers the operator,
then waves at the surveyor
with his neon vest.
For days they have been
wandering through the village
and the mayor
lets events develop as they will.
He sports the burden of his heavy office
like everything across the square,
and greets the onus gushing
with his scouts' cheer:
his trash collectors and the adjutant
of the newly barracked company of grenadiers.
Aerobic lessons for mother and child
will take place, as an exception, open-air.

IV.

On the widescreen at The Lion,
the hero canters in with his dispatches
back into the Middle Ages.
His message muffles
the chatter of the Trucker's Union.
The president is the only one
watching.
In the entrance, the landlord
fills up his register
as outside, a boy
counts the axles on a haulage truck,
and at the carpenter's table,
the grandson gets a smack around the head.
Grandpa believes in targeted beatings.
Where we live on the land,
the church is still the village!
It reflects in the façade
of the new administration building,
its high-baroque angels draw close attention
to the HR department on the third floor
where before each layoff,
the boss is crucified thrice.
Midday and night
an auxiliary policeman
coordinates the traffic before business.
Put off the catastrophe,
the saying goes.
He's always alone
on his way home.

V.

Little sexual activity
these past days,
visibility is excellent:
an inauthentic wind.
A woman hides the broadcast from B_ _,
and the storm under the bed has passed.
In the upper valley, two model-airplane enthusiasts
are taking up the fight.
Air strikes from the center of the sun,
an oak-wood body painted with love,
and a Union Jack on the lacquered balsa surfaces.
A marching band toots on the transistor radio
of the ground crew:
Nevertheless, with an itchy trigger finger
he scribbles on what was sprayed pale blue in the morning:
D E S I R E
Crap, says the station manager.
A teacher pleads for a whole sentence.
A bird in the hand
is worth two in the bush;
but they never learned that,
suggests the tardy pharmacist.
He carries his peculiar bright blue pill
outside the normal assortment.
And not a soul asks the jubilarian
with the golden pocket watch
for the time.

VI.

Broken wisps of condensation
draw themselves lengthwise over the sky.
The wind spins old leaves
through the streets.
A woman with a heavy heart leaves the market.
A white Pontiac is doing
its rounds in the village.
He's waiting for that eighteen-wheeler
with the wide tires
and the halogen cannons.
The air vibrates in bass lines
above his car roof.
Dust scatters
from the carpentry shop.
In the neighboring village, they're saying
the streets are
already under water.
Two lads, in anticipation of Lyon,
are on their best behavior.

The long-distance drivers depart.

Overgrown Gardens

Unpublished poems
from around the time of *Life on the Land*

Cogwork

I let myself be wheeled around,
someone supposedly said.
It's the only salve
for these abysmally sunny afternoons—
considering also the squeals of the gamboling kids,
the happy toot-tooting of the overland drivers
on their sympathetic car horns.

It's no laughing matter,
when even with questions asked,
answers are not to be expected
from the radio sermon on Sundays,

or when even your fist
no longer
fits your pocket:
Yes, yes, those beautiful moments
no longer suffice,
and a refrain comes to you
that's good enough to weep to
and the bread for your brothers
molds in the oven.

I promise myself none of the above
to start a conversation with you.
I knew my sentence by heart long ago.

Or do you see yourself as irresistible?
Have you still not figured out
that your eyes glow like that?

I call that seeing irresponsibly
when your surroundings irrespectively
mirror in the apple of your eye:

high voltage power pylons, four-lane highways,
red and white traffic cones, meadows,
or letters to the editor on an open field
slowly getting snowed under.
Oh, the surprising arrogance of the letters
that repeatedly come together as words:
faint-hearted, skyward-bound,
Wittgenstein Castle,
sperm-bank:

the church's weekly circular, bulk-mailed,
but deeply personal.

Dry Season

We speak to the fishes
at the silt microphone.
They count as the most attentive listeners.
As long as the gills still glow crimson,
the scaly suit sparkles.

Without the fish state of affairs,
with their withering geraniums for ears,
it might still be possible;
but for the likes of us, the deluge
(we who admire the Fall)
is indispensable.

No one comforts you,
aside from the passing cruise ships
filled up with the leftovers
of Occidental travel agencies,
and to top it off,
and that these days,
any tidal shift
is expected in vain.

M.

Sometimes you are a mountain, Brother,
that trembles and bubbles
on the inside.

Your breathing falls abruptly.
Melodious vapors cleanse you
right between your teeth.

They aren't eulogies;
you even inhale your shivers
as if you possessed them.

Sunday in the Country

After a long winter
at last the sockless days.
Whomever dwelt behind the mountain
now reappears.
Nights are mild.

In the moonlight
on the market square,
a ring of sawdust lazes
between beer crates,
and ice trickles.

But all around the dance floor
they still don't stop
leaning against each other,
even though the local wrestling champ
guided his prize calf home long ago.

Boat Hire

1985

A Humble Day's Work

Wasps and old wives
linger in the air.
My neighbor
fills up his silo
for winter.
I lay my hand
on your breast.
He who contends his life,
maintains it is true.
Something I just appropriated.

A Sketch

Contrary to noticing
the quickening punctuation of my pulse:
when everything tumbles about
in its nothingness, I wait
until the oscillation of the symbols
rushes back into the eye.

Missive While Walking Tall

1991

Music School

My preference is for the music of those
who can do nothing
with their peers.
Just like Ignacio L.;
the wings of his baby grand embrace
the borders of South America,
even when he plays Schubert.
And the children listening in
all wear their
glasses too large
to witness how Ignacio
sings from within.

Expedition

Waiting on the carpet's
snow flurry
on a green background.
Waiting until the windows
have steamed up,
the seasons discernibly
peel away from the walls
and the view clears
over Newfoundland.

Outpost

Devotions on the horizon,
a cubbyhole for our
godson.

Nirvana Mattresses
was the name on the brochure
carried to us by the wind.

Whiteout

Cuddly animal show
on a Sunday afternoon. Rain.
We witnessed the breeder's
lack of qualifications.
A little retouching on the fur
of the milky-white rabbit
became the condemnation
of that gentle man.
It cost him,
we heard,
his living.

Backlight

Black sediment is the condition
I notice early in the morning.

Through the wooded brushstrokes of the hills
the morning sun shines her searchlights
under the hemline of the pines.

When day begins, I always
do a handstand in front of your bedroom door.

Eyebright

Read
and note:
you are understood
by the words. From time to time.

Counter-Encounter

To see in the looking-away.
To hear in the listening-away.
To recognize, what, even
by demonstration, does not
become visible.

II.

OUT OF EARSHOT
(1992–2003)

Short Announcement

1995

Continuation

Flight

Pushing off with our arms,
we fly for nights
through the environs.
Our starry guards
light the way.
They discovered the grave
of a young child
from the Paleolithic
praying on the wings
of a swan. That flight
sent us forth.

State of Affairs

We jolted awake
to the sound of porcelain
teeth smashing.
Also the other
objects in the room,
vases, paintings,
are just no longer
there.

Their furtive presence
may at any time cap-
size by sheer
force.

Visit to the Countryside

Autumn wind inflames
the deciduous trees.

The stepmothers
stand in a circle

and all the stones
carry their names.

Sideshow

Snails have
inscribed the stones: *PAX*
written in a cursive script
on the edge of the garden, the letters
sparkle. No place else
with such assurance,
so legible. Come,
lick the salt
from my hand!

Kirchberg

A cow places
its face on the udder
of another cow.
The bells chime.

Songbirds fly
off the landlady's
broom handle.

North Train Station

Between incoming trains
the locomotive operator in blue overalls searches
for his composition.
A sad song melts
underneath his tongue.
Through his walkie-talkie he's in touch
with his world: *Decouple,*
she orders him. And he does.

High Noon

The subway train roars out of the city
into a dark tunnel. Two passengers
knot their legs together in the middle aisle
and take their fingers on a walkabout.
His breath steams up her red fingernails.
Their birthmarks flicker. But shortly before the next stop, the
woman's teeth begin to rot, the man's hair falls out,
and a blind man plummets into
the open gangway.
      Arriving in Austerlitz, the couple
decide to return to the city in separate trains
to find salvation at the office again.

Flaubert's Grandchild

A blue sky moves over the construction lot;
the allure of the firewall is striking. A Jacobin
woman with a shopping bag and a dog conquers
the farmer's market, the delivery man sings his egg-
plant song.
       A three-year-old stands on the corner; he
takes note of everything he hears and sees
in his yellow notepad. Mother is waiting.
She knows reality is ungraspable, except,
perhaps, with a pencil in your hand.

Evenings in Atlantis

A water nymph surges
in long strides over the piano.
The barmaid's cleavage glows
out into the Atlantic.
The wall frescos
waver.

Here the learned church painter
really pitched in
with his paintbrush, exalts
the lady behind the counter. We
resign ourselves wordlessly
to their demise.

Break-Fast

A salty odor edges in,
the ocean elbows into the room,
the snow blowers back off.

Once again, anything is possible
until it isn't. A strange breathing
commences behind my ears.

Personal Arrangement

Geography: Twelve Haiku

In Verona

On the farm lane,
a couple approaches me.
The lover limps.

Outside Bologna

The hunters are planted
in the meadow. They're waiting for
the mercy of the wild.

Toward Ravenna

On the surface
of the sky, a mosaic
shows your face.

Stopover in Rimini

A sprig of lavender
falls into the cabin. We spin
a fig leaf in the wind.

Arrival in Dublin

We had to ask folks
for directions because they were
so beautiful when they talked.

A Rind of Tilsit

Above the cemetery,
it smells of cheese. Perhaps
there has been a mix-up.

Oklahoma, USA

Out of the afternoon's
gray hip,
your word: *evening*.

Hammerfest, Norway

Straight through the plains
of the hiker's hair parting,
true north.

Tibet

Evenings I lie at the foot
of the mountain range and bite
into a pillow made of stone.

In the Camel Train

This long road,
up on your own
legs, day by day.

High Atlas

Light shoulders
demonstrate how the earth
may be carried like a balloon.

Beautiful View

To peer into the grass,
to clench one's teeth:
don't mix up the verbs!

A Russian Trip

A toothless elephant
stares into the skylight.
The dodecaphonist raps
her fingers on the desk.
The piano has been pawned.
We ladle out the soup
fearlessly fast.

Mother Nature

There were days
we wore our trousers
inside out—to out-fox
the lightning; who, we knew
wanted to smack that bad boy
straight in his tight-lipped mouth—all
at Mother Nature's bidding.

Yarn

2000/2002

Dragonflies

She Fly

Ma S'Quito insisted she remain an insect for a lifetime. *One day I'll sprout wings and vanish from here.*

On an unexpected Tuesday, when everyone was at work, the time had come, the sixty-five-year-olds had to be hoisted out, four-winged, shimmering, here and there, but insistent—in her compound eyes the world mirrored in all directions—and she flew out to the pond to be with her fellow-kind.

Official Announcement

Yes, Mrs. Jaun, I admit it, since this morning the 2nd of April, when I initiated the bankruptcy case against you, and you visited me personally to discuss a debt-restructuring moratorium, I haven't had a wink of sleep. On my part, I too have unexpectedly fallen into bankruptcy. In short, I was taken aback on the spot by your uncanny resemblance to my wife, with whom I have been married over twenty years; mostly happy ones. Everything that binds me to you is almost fated from that first encounter, and has confounded me to such an extent that I shall now require—as a reality check and in order that we might both find a way back to ourselves again—to kindly request on my part a moratorium: would you grant me, for the duration of the proceedings, to inconspicuously rest gently by your side?

In America

The shark from the TV movie earlier this evening now hangs as an unfortunate carp on the fence. (How reality always reports back to dreams and wonderfully recalibrates itself!) And the waiter's tattoo at the hotel bar traversed the toothless mouth of the Amish man who spoke my own Swiss dialect—both our ancestors hail from Emmental. And how this same language we had in common, our encounter—after that small accident (my car slid backwards into your willow fence and managed to squash your carp)—was hassle-free: Even the large dog and the other animals in that foreign yard listened in!

Lucie (on earth)

It was on the evening of September 2nd we both acquired new names—after a quarter century of having taken *Coo-Coo, Teeny-Weeny,* or any number of names carefully into account.

I swear it, we never gave away our secret, even during our travels, when a *Darling* or *Buttercup* would spontaneously flow from the tongue as if by itself. And we never stood before our growing children as *L'il Bear* or *Mouse.*

When Lucie turned fifty, a branch broke from the willow tree in our backyard. We chopped it into kindling, then went back into the house. It was late at night when Lucie first spoke of a "sign." She stood motionless in front of the mirror, night cream in her left hand, her right placed on a couple of wrinkles on her neck. I was waiting for the late night news, but Lucie insisted.

Oh my girl, my girl, I snuffled from the semi-darkness of the living room into the illuminated bathroom. True, I was likely somewhat inebriated, but was certainly imbued with a sense of well-meaning to console Lucie from a distance about the "sign" of the times, as it were. The jar of cream hit me straight between the eyes.

I didn't create the world, I suggested to Lucie angrily, dizzily, and pressed the cold base of my champagne glass against the throbbing bridge of my nose. The light came on. Lucie threw herself at my feet on the parquet, quite naked, and spoke into my empty glass as if it had been a microphone: *I'll console you too, out of love, my boy,* she said.

From the Cryptic Dictionary of Future Literature

I want to be your publisher, said the black-clad fellow, and placed his hand on the young poet's knee.
>   She struck him with her glove on his fingers
and agreed:

Get rid of the dog!
>   Immerse your handkerchief in the sea!
>   Bang on the drum!

A book tour in the United States followed:

On-Campus Poem
>   *My habit of sitting cross-legged on unheated radiators:*
an epigone stud farm

The editor took notes (the readership applauded, in most cases four-handedly). In this fashion, they created an oeuvre together.

The Sponsors Drop In

Three men in gray suits entered the tower chamber. They came here to get Hölderlin under contract. I eyed them from below. They did not maintain eye contact, but nestled sheepishly around the double volumes that gave them a sense of security. The gentlemen drew deep breaths, a briefcase was at hand. Hölderlin turned away, pulled his bedcap over his ears. I pulled down his blinds.

Is it already closing time? asked an art connoisseur friend testily. They stumbled into the dark room, scraped their bloody noses up against the wall.

What's with the blind jealousy, gentlemen! I said softly as a subordinate, taking pity on these three dizzy gents.

Father's Secret

We harassed our father to no end to find out where Lalaport was. Over there, it was said (unbeknownst to us) he had conducted the mixed choir.

The road to Lalaport, sometimes referred to as Limburg, came to be known as so damned arduous (there were ears hardened by years of listening, but we waited patiently in front of the closed railway gates for hours on end) that we sank in our claws halfway there and the cremation requested in our father's will was immediately set in motion.

Art History

Charles Atan, a native Genovese; we met once again
Unter den Linden in Berlin. What a dude, Karl!
    In the seventies he lived (after his monochrome phase)
unflinchingly in the manner of Jackson Pollack. He swung about
wildly just like his paintbrushes, got the audience's attention with
his shrill whistle; but next to his easel on a scrap of card was written:
    Paint divas!

A Day for Erlenmeyer

The current owner of Albert Einstein's brain, a British physician, provided, as was recently noticed, his prized organ, at disposal for certain experiments.

Its comparison to the brains of 35 men and 56 women scientists established a few conspicuous anomalies in the Nobel laureates:

Alongside a rather rudimentary central Harrison groove (sulcus), they discovered in the lower parietal lobe, where it is accepted that the center of mathematical cognition resides, a gnawing trace of healing laughter.

In Helsinki

He wore a striped jacket, and to match his shoes, he sported a red, summery hat on his head, collected empty bottles and lived on Redemption in the outskirts of Helsinki. I discovered him in front of the window of a furniture store where he was surely comparing his wardrobe with the lime-green labels of the most expensive garments in that house.

As we then hunkered over a Polaroid, which we had playfully posed for together, after we sought conversation, he said, somewhat sheepishly, but in perfect English: *I prefer Latin.*

Haute Couture (1)

Balz lay in the arms of a green two-piece he had cut out of sheer force of habit from grass. From the second floor, Irma looked down at her husband and the large grass woman.

Stand up, Balz, stop joking around, she called down softly, but reproachfully. Balz didn't move a hair. He had already vowed earlier this morning to mow the lawn again before the first spurt in order to be allowed to remain undisturbed in his house. He simply lay there, draped over his newest cutting pattern: a birthday dress for Irma's eightieth birthday.

Old Masters

During the course of our wanderings through the city, we stumbled across an abandoned building at a crossroads. The night broke solemnly into the windows. A young man perched on the timber crossbeam and stared bewildered up into the sky.

Jesse, we shouted recognizing the young crucified carpenter who had worked for our former neighbor. His feet were already quite blue from the cold.

At least someone had to lead with a good example and persevere, proposed the supposed commander of this happening in the twilit hall, and dismissively shrugged off the two hunched-over characters who had a wool blanket draped over their collective shoulders, and who hung around near the oil heater.

We don't have to invent Christianity again, hissed the larger of the two women, who was paying attention not to spill the hot water between her legs as she infused the tea leaves. The other woman wept.

Don't move, said another male voice from the depths of the great hall. *I want to paint you like that, in anger, in frustration, and with that blue pot in your hand.*

Long Leash

East End, January 28

Just like every day, I
would love to have written
a great poem today. It would
have carried me on. For a while.
Instead; just noisy traffic
behind the windows, the neighborhood
rinses its dishes behind little walls,
and there's the crippling surge
of criminality. But,
we are versed in love,
the books say. The Pacific
and North Atlantic routes, the shipping
lines to Africa, ply between shopping
sprees. And in winter, the ice-cream van
doesn't halt for the children either.
The fruit of their native lands
shimmers through immigrants' plastic bags. Juices
run together in the mouth, around the eyes
and under the armpits. On the wide-
screen, the president shows off his
white cuffs. New continents
are forming on the horizon
where house plants are grown. It
goes on like that, steam rises from towers
and flower pots—until at 3 in the morning,
a blackbird gently rests her scales
against our window:
at that same time, the Emperor of China
squats in the kitchen and listens carefully
to his nightingale.

For Velasquez

Automobiles flare up
around the glade, red limos
with their golden ladies.
A hunter carries
his slain wild boar
straight through the dusty center of town.
Grass is greenish
on the slopes.

Haute Couture (2)

In the twilight
perched on the handrail,
we sensed a growing
levity.

She wore
a dress made
of bats' wings.

First November

The morning throws
a different light
on the milk bottling plant.

And I never saw
the sparrows sitting
so large against the sky.

But, my companion says softly,
Yesterday already succeeded
as a totally respectable day.

Second November

In the morning at three a.m., all
the railway gates in the country are lowering.
The traffic lights jump
to red.

Just here and there, an ambulance
finds its way
over the tracks.

Otherwise, the streets and squares
belong to stretches of railroad, the airspace
reaches toward daybreak, and the
dead slip into their shells.

Behind closed curtains
the sleepless quietly
take off their hats.

In the Level Field

Upon entering the grocery
department, the emotion
evoked by the tight grip on
the shopping cart gets noticed.

We should imagine
Sisyphus as providential,
says Camus.

Providential Moment

Mist rises
around the high perches.

Bird's nests in the pro-
pulsion engine of a grounded jet.

A soccer shoe lies
next to the kickoff spot.

Circus

The year changes
hands. We reach
into an empty
millennium,

balance for a while
on its edge, kisses here,
kisses there, the circus
riders sweat

and just begin to comprehend
(just as HB taught us)
that the arena is
older than the world.

Bookmark

Recently while shaving
those old scars from
1945 caught my eye. They had
already given up on that child
who risked taking his second step
rather late.
For a split second, I saw
the shadows of my
distraught parents appear
behind glass. Then, behind
the casket glass—I clearly
remember it—my brother's
face. Time, my
time, drew itself together
parabolically into two indentations
across my neck—and in the guise
of my own children
with their life cycles, their astonishments,
frustrations and laughter facing the world.
At night behind closed eyes
a book opened.
Under a pale blue
gauze, the line-drawing
of a uniform emerged. Within
the martial
men's apparel rests
(other way round) a human.
Above a photo of this naked
soul was written: *For us.*

Breath. Pneumonia. Foehn.

From the School of Life

1

On the farmsteads, foxes are lurking everywhere.
One steers clear of the bitten agriculturalists.
The hunters move to the city
and resume the hunt.

2

The School of Life begins at three
in the morning. At seven, mostly bagatelle.

3

Whomever has still not discovered sleeplessness,
that's their own fault. I always keep one eye shut
in the light. That's because of the night-blindness at the beginning
of a lecture.

4

The truth grasps at simple sentences;
one more pill after another slowly dissolves
in the mouth until abatement kicks in.

5

It is more pleasurable if everyone on the boat sinks.

6

They who are expecting,
insist on their own veracity.

7

Friendly villages rise upon the toxic waste: where
I was, this IT should be again.

8

The electrical industry proposes planting plums
instead of pears. A brand-spanking-new
natural documentary.

9

From the suburban kids' hutch, the bugle announces:
Death to rabbits! Death to rabbits!

10

My brother once wrote: One should have been
born old in order to die young.

11

A turncoat presses his face on to his own
mirror image. It feels divided.

12

Ant networks burrow under the skin.

13

Naturally, everybody dreams of a masterpiece
and rests on the seventh day.

14

A trade in hand finds gold in every land.
The post office offers commemorative stamps
on this theme.

15

With an eye on the zebra crossing:
G O *LIE* W A L K
BETTER B R O A D BAND

16

That can happen, the loser said, by the by,
and the winner is bleeding from the nose.

17

That feeling of belonging in open spaces
has hung on a nail for quite some time.
It should like to be worn from time to time.

18

His search for meaning increasingly equaled
those quadratic moles growing
on his rounded, naked butt.

19

Every morning our animal love walks barefoot
through the dog park.

20

To present the windfall to the downfall.
Without falter.

21

The guilty party wants to confess,
but no one takes his confession. Thus
they move on, heavily burdened as they are.

22

Cold burns upward from your kneecap.

23

In the corner of the bistro two giggling old folk
slip each other the world under the table.

24

There are cultural investigations being under-
taken on mundane germs. Snow lies
on car bumpers.

25

That insight into the thinking mind, while
shooting photos deep into the glowing ball of a sun.
It's only photos who don't lose their memory.

26

They who don't hit the mark with the
first shot are exposed to their companion.

27

Once again, those noises from
the irons clanking against each other. In the
coming night, I shall sink a shaft
into the very core of the earth's warming heart.

28

In the sled factory, snow hangs low from the
roof; the wrought iron is half-baked.

29

Even the experienced would love
to be described.

30

Behind the horizon, angels
are laying eggs on the atmosphere.

Passenger / Voyager

I

It's spitting on the panes. A young woman enters the compartment. She smells candied, like a bonbon. The lad next to her is salivating. He swallows and swallows, but shortly before we reach Imst, he can't hold back and begins to carefully lick her naked, browned shoulders.

2

A couple steps on in Singen looking for two seats. They help each other out of their jackets, whisper; glow from within. One hopes, spontaneously, to arrive in these latter years with such thoughtfulness and dignity. They are seated with their backs against the movement.

3

Love is more powerful than death, I read on passing a placard raised high behind a sturdy set of gaping graves as evidence thereof. My front man stares straight ahead; he sits on a provision of sand waiting on the Leipzig winter.

4

Between two gloomy forest plots, a hunter comes out of the closet. The scent of his aftershave finds its way right into my cabin: the huntsman swears by cologne for the prevention of tick infestation. He prescribed it in autumn 4711 to his hunt beater.

5

The poet K. tells us of his heart-diseased cat. He gets no shuteye at night and never leaves his house for longer than an hour. The heaviest burden, however, he adds, is the outrageous cost of high-tech medicine. I cover his taxi fare.

6

Almost in Constance. A woman is wearing a complete ocean liner on her chest: rope and anchor, winch, helm, sail, gyrocompass; but no one far and wide; the once-boarded now lost with her in the maritime twinge.

7

Every syllable an ejaculation. The young man speaks as if he were
rapping. The wheels rattle hard against the tracks. Looming smoke-
stacks on the horizon.
Instead of a head, his girlfriend grows a microphone
out of her neck.

8

Past Weimar. The deep sky hauls water bags over the fields. In be-
tween, like a counterfeit coin, the full moon. On the embankment,
the railroad staff appears as if conjured from ancient ballads.

9

A traveler majestically paces up and down the wagons with a green
tie knotted around his neck. He stares out of his one wily, minute
eye straight into the gawping eyes of his fellow passengers. *A poor, sick
man*, a mother explains to her child. The child would prefer to run
off with him.

10

A mermaid steps off the train, shakes out her hair. She slides her tail-
fin between her shoulder blades and slips along the train windows
in the direction of the city. The platform and the train station are
already submerged.

11

Godfather on one cheek, Adam on the other. The spark leaps over the gap, a tat-
tooed man explains. And looks quite like Michelangelo himself.

12

The conductor punches holes diligently with his left hand. I would
like to finally see a deer romping in the glade. Instead, in the breaking
dawn, soccer teams scurry over all the hills.

13

A young woman says farewell to her boyfriend. Steps on to the train
all-alone. For a split second, the skin vanishes from her face.

14

A woman praises the artificial geraniums while coasting past. *Nowadays they can't be distinguished from the real ones; however, it's very important,* she adds, *not to leave the plants in front of the window.*

15

My dark-haired companion hums an oriental song, softly. After Uster, a desert stretches behind the train windows. Dunes wander, and the caravans head home.

Breath. Pneumonia. Foehn.
Counting Breaths for a Natural History Museum

Our ancestors were hunters.
They bequeathed us their hunting blood.

I

The first chamois killed in Aargau,
released in June 1959 at Villiger Geissberg,
was erroneously shot in November 1959; her
glass eye still gapes into the basement.

2

It's probably 1968, and Günther Eich
(on a Tuesday) reads in the main hall
of the museum for future moles and his
poems.

3

In case of fire,
please observe the regulations:
Contact the fire department.
Save people.
Latch doors.
(Monday and Wednesday: fixed hall reservation
by the anthroposophists)
Fight fire.
Call the animals by their name.

4

The flugelhorn bumps up
against the trumpet. The jack-
hammers pull ahead.

5

On the top floor, it's
the central island that first crumbles
to dust; its artificial grasses wither.

6

Between elk heads,
a second-hand edges ahead,
and the majestic beasts come forth
from the walls.

7

In the mouth of the Indian tapir,
the tongue vivifies.

8

The formalin level sinks.

9

Quietly the great
showcases break in two;
the groaning of the lizards
reaches our ears.

10

Wind rolls
through the hallways, and mixes
with the wild farts
of the pigs:
Pneumonia.
Breath.
Foehn.

11

The camphor balls from the birdcage
roll away in the direction of the train station.

12

Bearded vultures,
secretaries,
cranes,
raise their heads.

13

Beware
the bull-headed
shrike!

14

The offending hunter
takes back his shot,
watches the chamois graze
in the gloaming.

15

Oregon announces
the arrival of the beavers.

16

The anthroposophists distribute
watercolors in order to
extinguish the burning horizon.

17

The brown-throated three-toed sloth
asks directions for the fastest way
to reach South America.

18

Marsupial bat.
Wombat.
Giant clam.

19

Go down
on one knee
before the capuchin monkey!

20

With flecks of gold from ostrich eggs,
the tiger diligently colors in
her bleached fur;
and for anyone
who wants to see it,
shows them her bite.

21

Brain coral.
Dustbin-lid jellyfish.
Diplozoon paradoxum.

22

The elephant carries home
his ancestors' mountains of bone.
On the outmost rib,
swallowtails quiver.

23

Something's moving under the carpet.

24

Standing upright,
the gorilla and the orangutan
shuffle upstairs. It's only now
Günther Eich recites the last lines
of his last poem:

"... the world doesn't end,
is something you must learn."

Lions Lions: Reflections of Venice

2004

PEOPLE CLIMB
the arched bridge and freeze
for a moment at the zenith:
some caress each other, others gaze
down pensively at the elopement in the canals.
Others tighten their arms
around their handbags, grasp rails
and dive down the other side of the bridge,
back down to street level.

SHE WEARS A PALE BLUE that reminds you
of former East Germany, whereas the groom,
in his sheer shirt, holds his blooming white tie
up to the gray sky. This not-quite-so-young couple,
wandering hand in hand through the rain-
soaked city, appear not so unhappy to
be about town, and fear no weather patterns.

"I'VE SPENT MY BEST YEARS hunting mosquitoes to spare the elephant," the early arrival says to the barkeep, and makes a face like the sombrero-wearing Ernest Hemingway in the photo he shows me of Ernest next to Guiseppe Cipriani on the island of Torcello. Meanwhile, in front of the restaurant, spring curses autumn on a winter's day.

FULL MOON. The skipper with the large
hi-fi system built in his prow coasts ahead.
He fills streets and squares with his
basses and feral song.

IN THEIR LAPS,
the Angels of Stan Stae
carry their bedding as clouds.

DURING THE DAY, when between
St Marcus Square and Arsenal, two warships lie at anchor,
the Venetians reach for their winter gear.
On Campo San Rocco, in front of the giant
show windows, a wandering minstrel tries it on
with his own interpretations; he even has that Mani-Matter
song in Italian in his repertoire, but people bustle
past, squeeze their hands deep in their pockets,
deep in their own songs and suffering, absorbed
in their own daily affairs.

   "Will it snow tomorrow?" the musician asks
and nods his head at two passing furs,
scrutinizes the sky and maintains the three
stone-faced holy men on the parapet
of San Rocco, while listening to his guitar solo,
moved their feet a smidge over the edge of the roof.

   In the 12th century it once snowed in Lacona
on the island of Elba during August. Because of their fears, the cit-
izens built a church, where, for eight
centuries, it reads: *Madonna della neve.*
She still waits pensively.

   "Yesterday all my troubles seemed so far
away," the singer croons. Tourists roll by
with their suitcases, while the saints on the roofs shut
their eyes on command.

   A daisy-chain of handsome mainland women
steers laughing toward the Campo. From beneath
the open cloak of the young Madonna, her
warmed, glimmering, unfrosted, mustard-colored,
tanning-salon November-belly emerges.

THE DREAM HANGS

old burdens on me. I carry them
in my worn-out pockets
through the city at the crack
of dawn. And always, around
that same time, this pair walks
toward me. His wrinkled child
greets me, serenely.

IT'S NOT TOO GLOOMY
for Maria on her cloud, rising
from the *terra firma*.
Beseeching in their many-colored
vestments, longingly clinging
to the sky, rank and file remains:
With her warmed calls toward
the Assumption, it helps
that the air actually carries them.

SOMMOZZATORE is proud of his fastest boat,
Frogman. Stakes and jetties teeter, the water
cowers, cuts in, flushes out, then recedes:
to give in is the law of the lagoon. In close proximity,
a woman waves from the window of a palace.

IT DIDN'T SURPRISE ME

Father called today on this bleary
December day. And Venice still
displays herself in the window,
this inexhaustible city. On the telephone
I would use the word, "Serenissima."
Father would spell it out loud later
and no one would hold it against him.
A Venetian, whose Venetian soul
listened in by chance, possibly walked toward him,
corrected him in a friendly fashion: *Se-re-nissima.*
They broke into conversation,
(some form of Esperanto as it would be
spoken among those of a similar disposition).
Even Mom chuckled. And my brother, alienated
after the first few words, beamed
from his entire face:

In this way, on this winter's day,
I made new friends up in heaven, and
promised to distribute those wild and
well-travelled kisses to these, our own
grown up children, and also to my
adoring wife who divides our
organic way of life—the bright
days and the labyrinthine pathways,
the floods and the crucifixions,
the flight of the angels throughout
the city—and who, under her icy
rule of law, makes us raise our cups
to the screech of the seagulls.

Out of the Dust

2010

Dream Leftovers

Pinacoteca

Clouds roll
adamantly by and light
rain falls, falls.

One woman pours
milk, the other
combs her hair—for
three hundred years:

Not life, said
Malraux, but the statues,
will be our witnesses.

Summer of a Century

Through the shutters,
observing the summer,
its dusty fur.

(A cosmetics salesman adjusts himself
in front of the hairdresser's door,
waistband and tie.)

Grasses wither beneath
the fiery wind.
Tar blooms black.

Wiepersdorf, *later*

I

The wheel hums quietly across the plain,
glides along the shadow axis
of the warrior king. Large
passageways, small crowns. Larks
and falcons are in the air, bow
and arrow. Day's paleness sinks
behind the satellite's village, people
stand in front of houses that streak past.
Later on the edge, the carcass
of a rabbit still fleeing. Wind
and cloud roll off and away.
In the front yard, the dwarf
reaches for his shovel and digs
a hole in the Marchigian sand
for August Ziekert, forest ranger, off-duty.
Goes by the name *Wolf*. He freed grandmother
and child from that animal belly. The flagstones
of the Wiepersdorf boulevards
are now covered in asphalt.

2

Everywhere the mushrooms are ready.
A glut, say the arriving Swiss,
and reap admonishment
from the Saxon forest ranger.
In autumn it withstands
little deviation—but we also
could never have expected, within
this youngest millennium, that your
most-loved daughter would return
to you out of the war.
In between you were gifted
serenities and a drum
in the ear which no one
touches, thank God.

3

The waxing and waning light,
the wandering cloud-shadows,
the dizzying wind.
Once again, day plays a butterfly
I know into my hands, dragonflies
hunt over the abandoned
nuclear-warhead warehouse in the pine forest,
the duck squadron takes off.
Every blink an image. The hypo-
glycemic light drives the sweat
from my skin. With cold fingers
I record the nail-
biting event.

Big Business

E Flat Major

We hear the musicians
age: they transform their
impermanence into tones
and reconcile us in time.

Indian Summer

They bash my summer hat,
the acorns. A hunter dangles
from the tree. The woodpecker drums
for his insects, stoically.

Preparatory She-Night

Preparatory She-Night

Sometimes before day arrives,
my life becomes accessible
deep down
into my childhood.

Scars glimmer on
a verse: I cool them down
with rain, with snow.

Future remains fleeting,
only the dead are close
and the future looses
its consequence.

—for E.B.

Light

There are sentences
which heal

and days
lighter than air.

There is a voice
that I recognize

even before
it calls me.

—*for S.*

Three Conversations With Oneself

I

It's on the rise. From day to day. The chill
of the cloud formation, the heavy traffic. Yesterday
the grass was still green, just admit it, you
with your blue-and-black eye!
No clue about snow and even less so
about snowing. Will you finally pull your finger
out of the fringes, place the mushrooms on the table and
admit our defeat: we with our
black chanterelles just can't snow.

2

For days that creaking of the radiators
hangs on my ear as a warning.
And the pigeons with their messages
of a last precedence are doing their rounds
in the district. Still, if I dare
to move towards the window just once, the world
would eat straight from my hand.

3

Snow,
snow up to
the Austrian
Almighty-God-corner.
Our poor souls float down:
wet snow.

Expedition

Went in circles
for weeks, always
during the afternoons. Yesterday
he came to the gate,
said
he could now
visualize it again:
men formed
out of dust.

Out of Earshot

Towards midnight a yodeling
moped driver zips
past my window
with his visor open, as if
he were going off to a happy war.

Why then, a little later,
does the noise
of my burning cigarette paper
terrify me?

Ascension

We climb the old
processional route, uphill—
the cows graze, hornless
and still. Suddenly the brown one
raises her head, the bells chime.
Transformation! A Turkish couple
step out of the pines: "Ho!"
greets the man. His wife
lowers her eyes. (At this time
in Beromünster the Savior
is being raised up into the
rafters.) It's burning behind the forest—
in his baseball cap and his apron,
the Sunday chef tends his
sausages, sneezes: "Help me God!"
calls his guest. A motorbike
chainsaws birdsong.
Traffic jam at the Gotthard Pass,
the radio advises. On the Wyna,
a bottled message rushes
downriver towards the Rhine:
"By Whitsun your heads
should be navigable!"
the Lord promises.

III.

AN AUDIBLE BLUE
(2013–2016)

Unexpected Development

2013

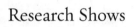

Research Shows

Regulations

We put off the research
until nighttime.
Between two and four
in the morning, a breakthrough.
During the day the office remains shut.

Research Shows

The master is badly beaten,
his heart is sadly searing.
He shows his randy teeth
and chomps the candied dog.

Core Business

It's all about the re-
patriation beneath the definition.
To arrive in unadulterated
conster*nation.*

Currency Exchange

A yearning for
the courtyard of the Lord
followed the fury arising from
courting the Lord.

Exchange Rate

From the bright light
behind the apparition
the poem recounts.

Miscellany

A lonely prediction
followed on the heels
of a great bene-
diction.

Then he fell
into the clutches
of his fingers,
into the arms
of the illness.
He suffered like an animal
and felt
more alive
than before.

Passive Resistance

He remained
sluggishly
present.

Attestation

Toward evening
as the songbirds go silent,
once again, I ask
the words to return to me;
to become or un-
become
what was.

Jaunt Around the Cliff Face

Through the Valley of a Hundred Valleys

Birch trunks glow
in a rambling green,
stretches of cable wobble.

But first, at the rail station in *Re* _ _ _,
the even-footed conductor
fetches his kingly orders:

Even today, his skyward glance
gives nothing away
about the hour of our death.

And again, we dive dizzily
deep into the thicket.

Into the Rose Garden

Rain falls and sniggers
through the world's
cemeteries.

We ask the innkeeper
for a jug
of ordinary
ancestral water
and also happily
leave a gratuity.

And the penny
under the tongue
has it covered.

Hereditary Stroll

Walked for a while
in Father's shoes
along the lakeshore.

And bent down
here and there following
poor advice along the way.

Because he couldn't
do otherwise.

Passau

On thin soles we trek over
the cobbles
of the refugees.

They have left a solid trail
behind. For us.

At Mondsee

Night hauls me
through adversity.
Limbless swimmers
line the lakeshore path;
the great cymbal
rattles from the sky.
I fruitlessly seek
to shed light
in the somber composition.

Borderline

The gas stations doze,
the customs house is crumbling,
we switch countries.

I keep watch here, warns
a sign over there—
not a dog utters a peep.

Suddenly, a beetle causes
the Earth to slip:
seeking witnesses.

Jaunt Around the Cliff Face

Thinking oneself
into the stone.
Only the pulse
of eons in the ear:
gravel gravel gravel

Still Life

The world about me
is slowly running out of breath.
Still I inhale, without avarice.

And drive out that regard
for reality
which doesn't really exist.

A Precious Moment

Love Poem

The act of separation
held us together
a life long; please
stay the night.

Library

When approaching the spines
a hint of collective
philanthropy still brushes up
against me.

Nocturnal Harvest

Driveshaft at the fore,
the Big Dipper plunges
toward Earth,
the cart sparkles.
With the glow of my cigarette
I guide it home.

Stroll

Day after day
I stumble deeper
into a landscape
that cuts through me.

Successful Convalescence

Loyal friends, I say
to my bones,

caress my skin,
greet my innards:

I should like to keep with-
in the encasement,

in which also from the outside,
my heart beats.

—*For S.*

We placed an earthenware dove
on his chest before he
drove into the fire.

In the morning, the bird
rose red-glazed
out of the warmed ashes.

Helios Hauls

2016

Helios Hauls

With a rickety cart,
Helios cruised the streets
of the early fifties:
encumbrances, all manner of haulage.

Still today, from time to time,
he delivers my dreams,
brings light into the rearmost
rooms of my Cretaceous period.

Holy Night

To push off, forcefully
from the newspaper's edge
and sail out
upon the open waters
of an unwritten
day: from across
the shore, children
wave: they balance
a glass ball
in their hands, calling:
Look how it's snowing!

Everything

From the depths of space
Hubble uploads
its pictures for us.
Constellations, galaxies
of luminous dust:
Immense reverb-
erations of all our
human worlds—
the glowing
and the extinguished,
the departed
and the awakening
starlets.

Memorial

A water lily reminds us
of our stern father.
Green and razor-sharp
its shaft juts out of its
own scooped-out habitat.
It even cuts off its daughters'
and sons' most recent
complaints straight at the mouth.

In the Dusk

We looked down
from the balcony
into Mister Bonsai's garden,
into an old wizard's
green Rapunzel-realm:
It makes me horny,
you said.

Moody February

Two early butterflies
deceive us that spring is arriving.
The snowbells tinkle.
On the park bench
a pensioner melts away.

From Pole to Pole

Walked lifelong
on cold feet
through the lingering day.
Not until nighttime
did my soles become
soft and warm, and
my skin, a white-
hot bearskin.

Abutment

The wall fragments
stretch along the edge
of the looming gravel pit.
A wily eye adorns
its craggiest stone:

Perhaps the Cyclopes of Futility
have been here
at the plant during the night—
for their, for our
edification.

Coherent Methodology

Sometimes even the most
convincing arguments
for life and the world
evaded him—he had to
start searching all over again,
or he courageously gave in
to the inexplicable.

Migration

On his fingers,
my grandson
counts the planets.

We want to live
on Saturn, it also
serves as a carousel.

Gray and curled our hair
flickers through space.
Meekly we look

back at our
cramped home, grasp
each other by the hand.

THE AUTHOR

Klaus Merz was born in 1945 in Aarau and lives in Unterkulm, Switzerland. He has won many literary awards, including the Hermann Hesse Prize for Literature, the Swiss Schiller Foundation Poetry Prize and the Friedrich Hölderlin Prize in 2012. He has published over 35 works of poetry and fiction. His latest novel is *The Argentinian (Der Argentinier,* Haymon, 2009) and his recent collections of verse are *Out of the Dust (Aus dem Staub,* Haymon, 2010), *Unexpected Development (Unerwarteter Verlauf,* Haymon, 2013), *Helios Hauls (Helios Transport,* Haymon 2016) and *firm (firma,* Haymon 2019).

THE TRANSLATOR

Marc Vincenz is an Anglo-Swiss-American poet, fiction writer, translator, editor and publisher. He has published twenty books of poetry, including more recently, *Leaning into the Infinite, The Syndicate of Water & Light, Here Comes the Nightdust, Einstein Fledermaus, A Brief Conversation with Consciousness* and *The Little Book of Earthly Delights.* Vincenz's novella set in ancient China, *Three Taos of T'ao, or How to Catch a Fortuitous Elephant* is forthcoming from Spuyten Duyvil. Vincenz is also a prolific translator and has translated from the German, Romanian and French. He has published ten books of translations, most recently *Unexpected Development* by award-winning Swiss poet and novelist Klaus Merz (White Pine, 2018) and which was a finalist for the 2016 Cliff Becker Book Prize in Translation. Vincenz is editor and publisher of MadHat Press, and publisher of *New American Writing.*

Acknowledgments (continued from page 4)

Original poem titles and their first-edition publications:

Die Lamellen stehen offen. Frühe Lyrik 1963-1991. Haymon Verlag. Innsbruck 2011
Weiße Gedanken
(unveröffentlichte Gedichte 1963-1967)

„Unterwegs"
„Lied"
„Treibgut"
„September (1)"
„Ich sammle die Pupillen ..."
„In meinem Haus"
„Das Geschehnis"

Mit gesammelter Blindheit. Gedichte. Tschudy Verlag. St. Gallen 1967

„Nachts"
„Zu neuen Jahren"
„Frühe"
„Schiffbruch"

Geschiebe mein Land. Gedichte. Sauerländer Verlag. Aarau 1969

„Rückkunft"
„Eiszeit"

vier vorwände ergeben kein haus. Gedichte. Artemis Verlag. Zürich 1972

„Vorstunde"
„Abends"
„Hafenstadt"
„Exekution"
„Berufserfahrung"
„Axiom"

„Metamorphose"
„Liquidation"
„Schicht"
Abend für Abend
„Sommer-End"

Kurzwaren. Schweizer Lyriker 4. Zytglogge Verlag, Bern 1978

„Poesie"
„Schöne Erwartung"

„Mit Redensarten leben gelernt"
„Abschminken"
„Jahreszeiten"
„Abdankung"

Landleben. Gedichte. Editon Howeg. Zürich 1982

„Altweibersommer"
„Landleben"

Die Lamellen stehen offen. Frühe Lyrik 1963-1991. Haymon Verlag. Innsbruck 2011
Zugewachsene Gärten
(unveröffentlichte Gedichte im Umfeld von Landleben)

„Räderwerk"
„Trockenzeit"
„M."
„Ländlicher Sonntag"

Bootsvermietung. Prosa Gedichte. Editon Howeg. Zürich 1985

„Bescheidenes Tagwerk"
„Zeichnung"

Nachricht vom aufrechten Gang. Prosa Gedichte. Editon Howeg. Zürich
1991

„Musikschule"
„Expedition"
„Außenstation"
„Tipp-ex"
„Gegenlicht"
„Augentrost"
„Wider-Sehen"

Kurze Durchsage. Gedichte und Prosa. Haymon Verlag. Innsbruck 1995

„Flug"
„Stand der Dinge"
„Besuch auf dem Land"
„Nebenschauplatz"
„Kirchberg"
„Nordbahnhof"
„Hoher Mittag"
„Flauberts Enkel"
„Abends in Atlantis"
„Früh-Stück"
„Geographie. Zwölf Haikus"
„Besuch in Russland"
„Mutter Natur"

Garn. Prosa und Gedichte. Haymon Verlag. Innsbruck 2000

„Fliegerin"
„Amtliche Mitteilung"
„In Amerika"
„Lucie (on earth)"
„Aus dem kryptischen Lexikon der Gegenwartsliteratur"
„Sponsorenbesuch"
„Vaters Geheimnis"
„Kunstgeschichte"

„Ein Tag für Erlenmeyer"
„In Helsinki"
„Haute Couture (1)"
„Alte Meister"
„East End, 28. Januar"
„Für Velasquez"
„Haute Couture (2)"
„Erster November"
„Zweiter November"
„In der Ebene"
„Günstiger Augenblick"
„Zirkus"
„Buchzeichen"
„Aus der Schule des Lebens"
„Passagier"
„Atem. Pneuma. Föhn. Abzählvers für ein Naturmuseum"

Löwen Löwen. Venezianische Spiegelungen. Haymon Verlag. Innsbruck 2004

Über die Bogenbrücken
Sie trägt ein hellblau
Meine besten Jahre
Vollmond
Die Engel von Stan Stae
Am Tag
Der Traum hängt mir
Ganz geheuer
Sommozzatore
Es erstaunte mich nicht

Aus dem Staub. Gedichte. Haymon Verlag. Innsbruck 2010

„Pinakothek"
„Jahrhundertsommer"
„Wiepersdorf später"
„Es-Dur"

„Indianersommer"
„Zuzüsterin Nacht"
„Licht"
„Drei Gespräche von selbst"
„Expedition"
„Außer Rufweite"
„Himmelfahrt"

Unerwarteter Verlauf. Gedichte. Haymon Verlag. Innsbruck 2013

„Regelwerk"
„Aus der Forschung"
„Kerngeschäft"
„Kurswechsel"
„Wechselkurs"
„Varia"
„Dann geriet er ..."
„Passiver Widerstand"
„Beglaubigung"
„Durchs Tal der hundert Täler"
„Zum Rosengarten"
„Erbgang"
„Passau"
„Am Mondsee"
„Borderline"
„Gang um den Felsen"
„Still leben"
„Liebesgedicht"
„Bibliothek"
„Nächtliche Ernte"
„Spaziergang"
„Treue Freunde, sage ich ..."
„Wir legten eine irdene Taube ..."

Helios Transport. Gedichte. Haymon Verlag. Innsbruck 2016

„Helios Transport"
„Heilige Nacht"
„Alles"
„Gedenkstätte"
„In der Dämmerung"
„Widerlager"
„Schlüssige Methode"
„Launiger Februar"
„Von Pol zu Pol"
„Migration"

Thanks to the following editors for work included in this volume:

T Thilleman for *Out of the Dust* (Spuyten Duyvil Publishing: New York City, 2015).

Dennis Maloney for *Unexpected Development* (White Pine Press: Buffalo, NY, 2018).

Grateful acknowledgement is also made to the editors of the following publications in which some of these translations originally appeared: *Plume, Solstice, Trafika Europe Quarterly* and *Asymptote*.